KU-441-537

INDUSTRY IN
EUROPE

Mark Smalley

Wayland

EUROPE

Series Editor: Janet De Saulles
Book Editor: Rose Hill
Series Design: Bridgewater Design
Book Design: Jackie Berry

First published in 1992 by Wayland (Publishers) Ltd.,
61, Western Road, Hove BN3 1JD, England

© Copyright 1992 Wayland (Publishers) Ltd.

British Library Cataloguing in Publication Data

In case of query contact Bibliographic Services on
071 836 8911.

ISBN 0 7502 0190 8

Typeset by Dorchester Typesetting Group Ltd.
Printed in Italy by G. Canale & C.S.p.A., Turin
Bound in France by A.G.M.

ACKNOWLEDGEMENTS

Benetton 41; Chapel Studios 4, 19, 21, 37, 40, 44 (top); Eye Ubiquitous (Paul Thompson) 11, (Paul Seheult) 16, (Nick Wiseman) 23, (Frank Leather) 28, (Nick Wiseman) 29, 30, 32, (John Hulme) 33, (David Cumming), 39, Eye Ubiquitous/Sefton 43; Topham 25 (top), 26, 35; WPL 13, 17, 28 (top), 36, 44 (left); Zefa 3, 5, 7, 8, 9, 10, 15, 20 (both), 22, 23 (top), 24, 25 (bottom), 39. The cover and all interior artwork is by Malcolm Walker.

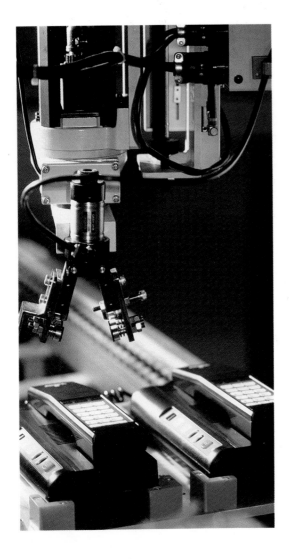

Contents

Introduction

Industry makes things. It produces the things we need and provides the services we use. This book looks at what industry is, and how it operates in Europe.

This book is itself the product of European industry. First, trees were grown, then they were cut down, pulped, and made into paper. That's the Scandinavian paper industry. The rolls of paper had to be shipped to Italy where the book was printed. The printing industry used precision machinery, made in Germany, to get the colour balance right on the photos. The chemical industry produced the ink.

France is famous throughout Europe for its fine wines. Here these bottles are being labelled in a French factory.

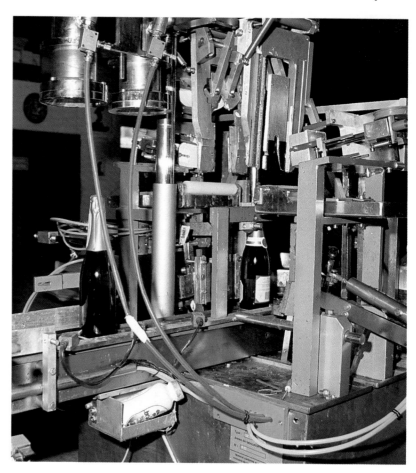

Timber is one of the most important industries in Sweden. Most of the sawn wood products, along with the pulp and the manufactured paper, is exported – chiefly to other European countries.

As you can see, a whole range of industries were used just to make this book. Think how many more industries are involved in producing really complex things like cars.

Industrial goods have to be sold. The profit made from sales means that industry creates wealth. Industry provides jobs for people making the goods, and indirectly it provides jobs for the people who sell those goods. Without industrial production, there would be nothing for shops to sell. Nor would there be anything to sell abroad to other countries. So industry is central to our way of life and to European society.

Europe was the home of the Industrial Revolution, when in the eighteenth century, machines were first used to increase dramatically the quantity of goods produced. Today European industry is going through many changes. Traditional industries like coal, iron and steel that used to employ thousands of workers are no longer as important as they once were.

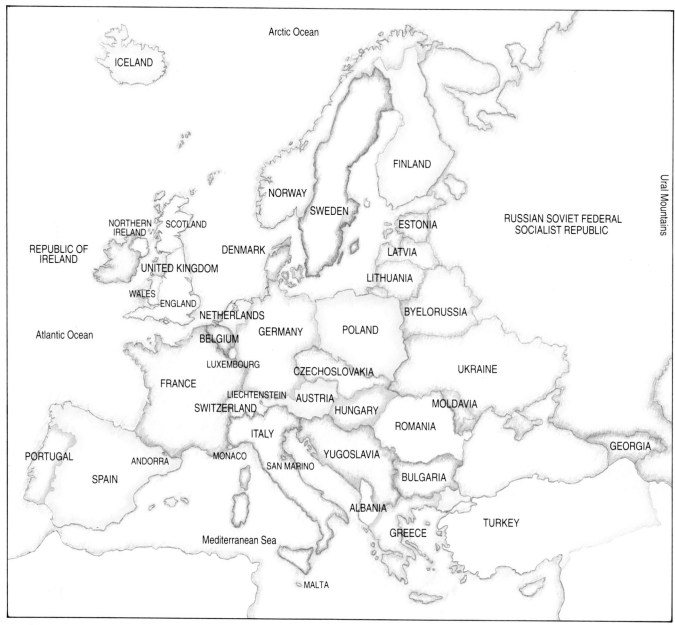

The new industries in Europe, for example electronics, are tending to use more high-technology, automated machinery and fewer workers. It has been realized that machines are cheaper to use than people. They work longer, produce more and don't complain. Making things as cheaply as possible means that the goods produced by European industry can compete with foreign products when sold abroad.

Europe itself is currently going

Above **The countries of Europe.**

Opposite page, left **How a product reaches the consumer.**

Opposite page, right **City businessmen.**

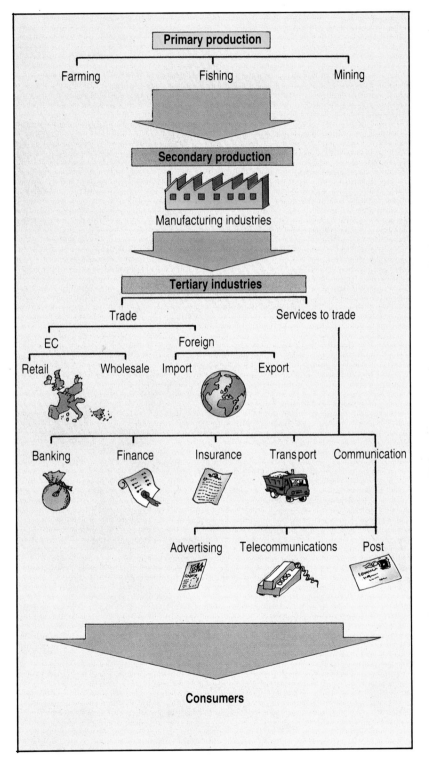

Primary production

Farming   Fishing   Mining

Secondary production

Manufacturing industries

Tertiary industries

Trade   Services to trade

EC   Foreign

Retail   Wholesale   Import   Export

Banking   Finance   Insurance   Transport   Communication

Advertising   Telecommunications   Post

Consumers

through a period of great change. In the USSR and Eastern Europe, society and industry are being reorganized. Their former Communist system no longer exists, and now they are seeing if the Western, capitalist system will work for them. It remains to be seen what form of government actually does work best.

What is industry?

There are three main kinds of industry: primary, secondary and tertiary.

Primary industry Fishing and mining are primary industries. They extract basic things from nature, from above or below the earth's surface, for example,

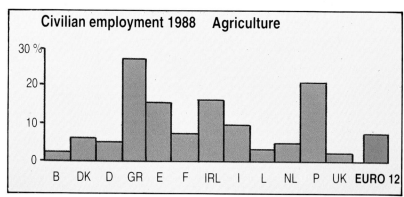

Civilian employment 1988   Agriculture

Opposite page
European industries are many and varied. Here, salt is being processed at a plant in Lanzarote, one of Spain's Canary Islands.

Right **Paper-making is an example of a secondary industry. This factory is in Dusseldorf, Germany.**

timber, fish, coal, metal ores, oil and gas. Farming is also a primary industry, where ground is put to use for the growing of crops or raising of cattle.

Secondary industry takes the materials provided by primary industry, and makes them into something else. This processing, or making of things, is called manufacturing industry. It is the main subject of this book.

Tertiary industry The third stage of economic development sees an increase in the number of industries that support manufacturing industry. Whilst manufacturing industry actually produces goods, the service industry (also known as tertiary industry) makes sure the goods are transported, stored, sold, and insured.

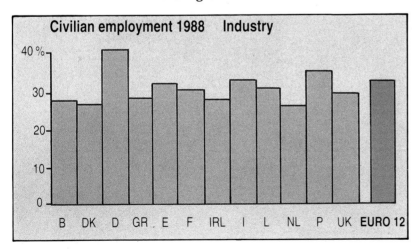

Civilian employment 1988   Industry

Commerce, banking, transport and telecommunications are all part of the service industry. Commerce is the activity of buying and selling goods. Banks allow businesses and individuals to borrow and store money. Transport moves goods by road, rail, air and sea from the manufacturer to the market, where things are bought and sold. Good, speedy telecommunications transmit information, using the telephone, TV and fax networks.

Some industries are run on a small scale. This flower-seller has set up a stall in the Grand Place Flower Market in Brussels, Belgium.

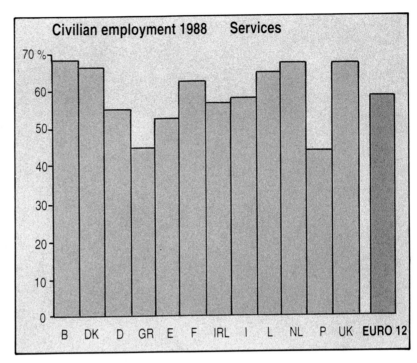

Civilian employment 1988   Services

The people who work in law courts, hospitals, schools and hotels are also part of the service industry. They provide a professional service.

The above bar chart shows the share of people working in the three different sectors of industry in the European Community. The service sector is the main employer, particularly in Belgium, the Netherlands, Denmark and Britain. Germany employs the most people in manufacturing industry. The EC's poorer countries – Portugal, Greece and Ireland – rely much more on farming than the others. Farming does not create as much wealth as either manufacturing industry or the service industries.

The pie chart below shows the percentage of wealth in the EC created by primary, secondary and tertiary industry. Agriculture provides only a small amount. Manufacturing industry provides one third. The majority comes from the service industries.

Above, left **Portugal relies heavily on its agricultural industry. These vineyards are in the Douro Valley.**

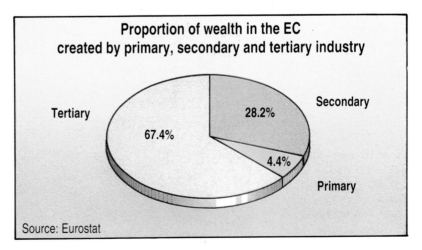

Proportion of wealth in the EC created by primary, secondary and tertiary industry

Tertiary 67.4%

Secondary 28.2%

Primary 4.4%

Source: Eurostat

Industry and economics

The total value of someone's belongings is called their wealth. Economics asks questions such as: how is a country's wealth made; where; who by; and what with? The economy presents a picture of the different areas in which that wealth is created and spent.

We can learn a lot by looking at diagrams of how wealth is formed and used. Fig. 1 compares the wealth of different parts of the world. The European Community (EC) is the second wealthiest region in the world.

Fig. 2 shows the population of different parts of the world. What does it mean that the EC is the second wealthiest region, with only the sixth largest population? It means that people in the EC are very much wealthier than those in many other parts of the world. If you divide the wealth of a region by the number of people, and

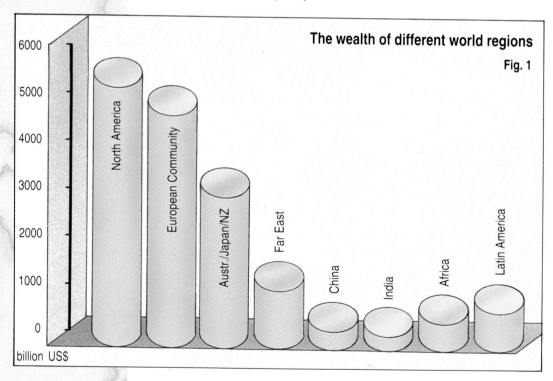

The wealth of different world regions

Fig. 1

billion US$

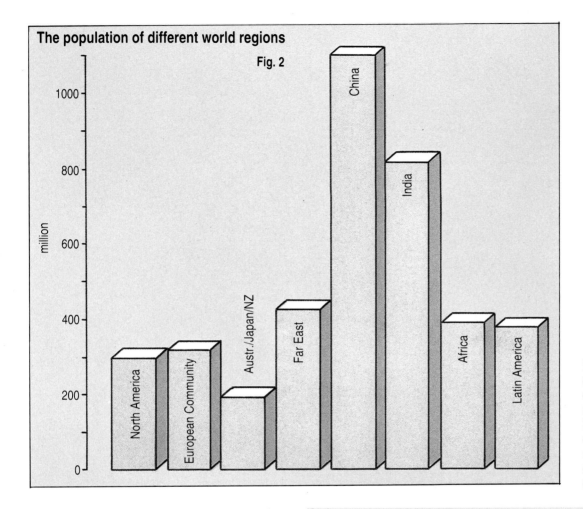

The population of different world regions

Fig. 2

million

- 1000
- 800
- 600
- 400
- 200
- 0

North America
European Community
Austr./Japan/NZ
Far East
China
India
Africa
Latin America

Below **An architect's design for a row of houses. The standard of living in Europe is high enough for many people to afford such accommodation.**

compare the answers with different regions, you will find out, for example, that a European is roughly 33 times richer than a Chinese person. Manufacturing industry has made Europe one of the richest areas in the world.

Fig 3. overleaf shows that more than two-thirds of wealth created in the European Community in 1988 was created by former West Germany, France, Italy and Britain. They are the EC's most industrialized countries.

Fig 4. lists the major manufacturing industries in the EC, and compares the value of the goods produced by them.

Although the basic iron and steel industry provides only 6.7 per cent of the money earned by European industry, metal goods are much more important if you consider how motor vehicles, ship building, tool-making and machinery all rely on the iron and steel industry.

HOW WEALTH IS MADE

Manufacturing industry processes the raw materials provided by primary industry. Processing something not only changes it, but also adds value to it. It becomes worth more money as a result.

A farmer might sell a 50 kg sack of potatoes to a crisp

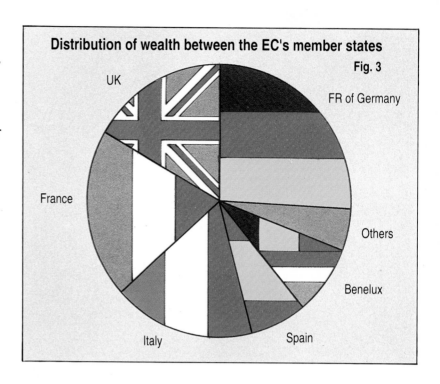

Distribution of wealth between the EC's member states

Fig. 3

UK · FR of Germany · France · Others · Benelux · Italy · Spain

manufacturer for £1. Turning the potatoes into crisps vastly increases their value. Three small 30 g crisp packs might then have

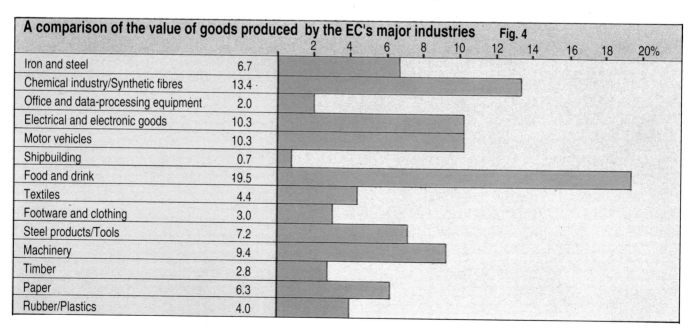

A comparison of the value of goods produced by the EC's major industries		Fig. 4
Iron and steel	6.7	
Chemical industry/Synthetic fibres	13.4	
Office and data-processing equipment	2.0	
Electrical and electronic goods	10.3	
Motor vehicles	10.3	
Shipbuilding	0.7	
Food and drink	19.5	
Textiles	4.4	
Footware and clothing	3.0	
Steel products/Tools	7.2	
Machinery	9.4	
Timber	2.8	
Paper	6.3	
Rubber/Plastics	4.0	

Scale: 2 4 6 8 10 12 14 16 18 20%

Steel panels being welded on to the hull of a ship at a German ship-building site in Hamburg.

the same value as one huge sack of potatoes. This is how manu-facturing industry creates more wealth than primary industry.

In the same way, Europe's manufacturing industries create wealth by processing raw materials bought from poorer countries. This is why industrialized countries are much wealthier than non-industrialized countries in the developing world.

The industrialization of Europe

The Industrial Revolution started in Britain during the period 1780–1820. Machines were introduced so that goods could be made faster, and in greater numbers than workers could manage with their hands. This process is called mechanization. The effects of mechanization were huge, and went far beyond industry. The Industrial Revolution can best be understood by comparing how things were before and afterwards.

Until around 1830 only Britain had begun to industrialize. A lot of wealth was created by the production and sale of cheap, mass-produced goods such as wooden and cotton textiles. Selling the goods abroad also increased the national income.

During the nineteenth century, Britain supplied much of the world with coal, iron and linen. Financial strength was soon turned into political and military strength. As Britain extended its control over many countries, so raw materials were taken from British colonies. Finished products, made in Britain, were sold back to the colonies.

Two English brothers, the Cockerills, went to Belgium in 1815 to demonstrate how machinery could increase production. The coalfields around Charleroi, in Belgium, were industrialized in a similar way to Britain: the technique of mass production soon changed the manufacture of Belgian iron, coal and textiles.

The north and west of France became industrialized around the coalfields of Lille, and in Alsace-Lorraine, close to Germany. Although many parts of the country remained rural, France had become a major industrialized nation by 1850.

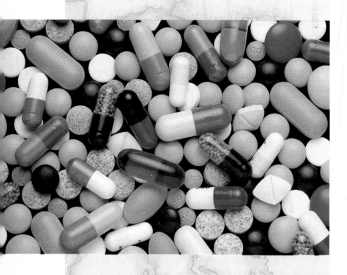

Today's industries: these pills were made in one of Europe's pharmaceutical factories. Each pill contains an exact balance of chemicals, regulated by highly sophisticated machinery.

The Industrial Revolution meant that large amounts of goods could be produced for less money than previously. The downside of this, however, was that working conditions were terrible, with child labour being common.

BE UNITED AND INDUSTRIOUS

AMALGAMATED SOCIETY OF ENGINEERS, MACHINISTS, MILLWRIGHTS, SMITHS, AND PATTERN MAKERS

As the Industrial Revolution drew on, various unions or societies were formed. The idea behind these was to protect workers' rights.

industrialized countries in Europe. The USSR and the Eastern European countries, however, did not fully industrialize until just before the Second World War, although they also have large coalfields.

Other countries, such as those in the south of Europe and in Scandinavia, lacked coal. The industrial development of countries such as Portugal, Greece, Sweden and Finland was made possible by the use of hydroelectric power after the 1920s, and by oil after the 1950s.

THE INDUSTRIAL REVOLUTION TODAY

Many of the basic lessons learnt during the Industrial Revolution are still in use today, although they have been changed to suit the ever-increasing use of machines. Take, for example, a washing machine. This complicated piece of equipment is made up of many parts. On a production line, people or machines are responsible for putting different bits of it together. Each person repeats one small task again and again, but between everyone, the whole machine is put together.

Organizing people in this way is called the 'division of labour' or 'specialization'. It means that unskilled people can learn their task very quickly, but it also means that the work is boring and

Germany did not really begin to industrialize until its many small kingdoms and principalities became unified in 1870. However, by 1900, the very important industrial region of the Ruhr had been established. Within 30 years Germany was producing more steel than Britain, and was the world leader in chemical production.

Because of their coalfields, Britain, Belgium, France and Germany became the major repetitive. Their work is being replaced by automated machines.

Mass production

Breaking jobs down into a series of small, specialized tasks enables each person to repeat his or her task very quickly. This leads to more things being produced in a shorter space of time. The use of machines also speeds up the process. Producing a lot of one thing in this way is called mass production.

Mass production resulted in a huge increase in productivity (the amount of goods produced by each employee). It also made it cheaper to produce goods. The increase in productivity was matched by an increase in sales. It created new wealth for the factory workers as well as the factory owners.

As the cost of mass-produced goods fell dramatically, more people were able to afford to buy more things with their wages. This, in turn, increased the demand for more goods by the public, starting a spiral of ever-increasing consumption which continues today.

Automation

Computers are now used to make machines produce more goods than if a person was in charge of them. This is called automation.

Let us take a machine tool such as a lathe for an example. It shapes metal, making the basic parts for new machines. Until the 1970s, lathes were manually operated. Gradually, workers in charge of lathes have been replaced by computers. These Computer Numerically-Controlled (CNC) lathes, as they are called, produce three times more goods than the worker could, and with greater accuracy.

Work on the production line today. Each worker here is completing one stage in the process of making circuit boards for use in the electronics industry.

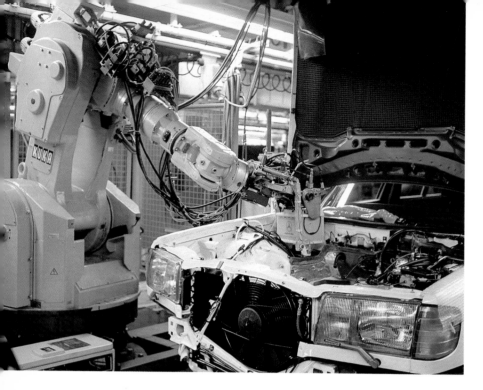

Above **This 'electronic arm' is placing a car battery in a Mercedes car. Do you think that it is a good idea that some jobs today are done by robots rather than people? What is the disadvantage to this?**

During the 1980s most European industries, such as the textile and car industries, began to use more automation and fewer workers in order to cut their production costs, and to increase their output and their profits. Otherwise, European products would not be cheap enough to compete on the world market with those from the USA and Japan.

Automated machinery can be designed to do many things. The Italian car manufacturers, Fiat, use robots to make thousands of spot-welds on car bodies. In the British company, Cadbury's, robot arms pack chocolates in the sweet factories, replacing the rows of people who used to do the same job.

Information technology (IT)

Information technology is all about the use of computerized information.

In Europe, France, Germany, Italy and Britain have led the field in developing IT. Companies in all areas of manufacturing industry are making use of IT to improve their performance, from the chemical industry to textile and car production.

Once the different departments of a company are linked by computer, information can then be gathered and compared. Using IT, managers can find out how much departments produce, how quickly, and at what cost. They can then decide to make improvements. IT is used to save time and money, and to increase efficiency and profits.

Right **Making money earn more money is an industry in itself! People working on the Stock Market rely on the use of computer technology.**

Industry's basic needs

This section looks at industry's basic needs, and how these needs have influenced the place chosen to build a factory or business. A new company needs: money to be invested in it; a source of energy to power the production of goods; a supply of raw materials to make goods; a workforce and machinery to make the products; transport to move the raw materials and finished goods. Finally, and most importantly, every company needs a market: without people who want to buy the finished goods, all the money and energy spent in making a product is wasted.

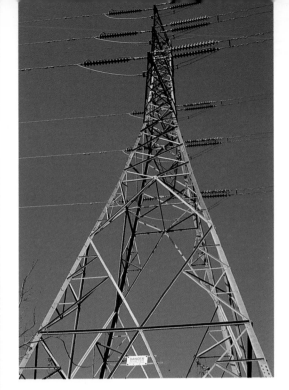

Electricity pylons link up Europe's power stations with industrial plants, where energy is needed for the manufacture of goods.

Money   A new company requires money to be invested in it. Machinery has to be bought, staff hired, a factory site built or rented.

Energy supply   During the Industrial Revolution, large quantities of coal were required to provide the energy for steam-powered machinery. Being bulky and heavy, the coal was very expensive to transport.

To cut transport costs, manufacturing industry came to the coalfields. This led to the growth of industrial regions like the North of England, and the Ruhr district in Germany. They were famous for the heavy manufacturing industries such as iron, steel, textiles and ship building: the traditional 'smokestack industries'. The introduction of portable energy, such as electricity, gas and oil, allowed some industries to move away from the coalfields.

The increasing importance of imported oil during the 1950s led to the growth of new industry around the ports and oil terminals where the oil was refined. This was how ports like Rotterdam in the Netherlands, Marseilles in France, and Milford Haven in Wales have become industrial centres. Many products come from oil refining, such as petrol, tarmac, petrochemicals, plastics, fertilizers and synthetic textiles.

Raw materials These are provided by primary industries, and processed by manufacturing industries. For example, trees are pulped and made into paper. Primary industries are often more common in Eastern European and developing countries than in Western Europe.

Western European countries such as Belgium, Germany and Britain used to provide and process many of their own raw materials. However, they have discovered that more money is to be made from buying goods that are already semi-processed, such as pure iron rather than iron ore. They then go on to process it even further, and turn the iron into finished goods such as parts for machines.

The labour force Many industries will set up close to cities so that they have a ready supply of workers, and a market for their product.

A shortage of workers after the Second World War led Britain to invite people from Africa, Asia and the Caribbean to go and live there. This was the beginning of Britain's multi-racial society. At the same time, France invited people from North Africa, and Germany invited Turks and Yugoslavs to go and work in their main industries.

People from the poorer European countries of Spain, Portugal, Greece and Ireland also went to work for their richer, more industrialized neighbours, and sent money home.

Rotterdam is situated at the mouth of the Rhine and Mass rivers and is one of the world's largest and busiest ports.

The way that industry has been run in Western Europe since the Industrial Revolution, through to the present day, has determined the way in which we live. This side of Europe has been market-led: this means that there has not been an overall plan for the way in which industry has developed, and that the needs of industry and profits have often been put before the needs of people. This has been done on the assumption that a thriving economy will automatically lead to wealth being filtered down to everybody, according to how much they are worth.

Eastern Europe, however, following on from the Russian Revolution of 1917, has held that market forces should be controlled by the State. In this way, products were priced according to what the State decided, not according to the quantity of production or the demand for the goods. Unemployment was virtually unheard of.

Today, Eastern Europe is abandoning its Communist principles. The system proved to be too vast and unwieldy. Beginning with Gorbachev's reforms in the USSR, countries such as Poland, Czechoslovakia and Hungary are heading towards a Western European style market economy.

However, the Western model is also far from perfect. Parts of the workforce might be used or discarded, according to the needs of industry. This can be heartless and lead to a state of confusion. Because modern industry requires a skilled workforce, young Western Europeans now spend longer in education, learning the right skills for the world of work. Yet industry no longer requires the entire population to be employed: unemployment in the West of Europe is very real and unlikely to disappear in the near future.

In the same way, at different times this century and according to the needs of industry and the state of the economy, women have either been encouraged or discouraged from working.

Left **A German miner (left) next to a Turkish miner. After the Second World War Germany expanded its workforce by inviting people over from Turkey and Yugoslavia.**

Below **Political changes in Eastern Europe have led to new developments in industry and trade. Today the importation of Western goods is encouraged, and advertisements such as this one are becoming increasingly common.**

Italy

In a sense, Italy is two countries. The northern half of the country is rich and industrialized. It seems closer to the industrialized North European countries such as Germany and the Netherlands than the south of Italy.

The south, known as the *Mezzogiorno*, relies much more on agriculture than industry as a form of employment. It seems closer to the relatively poorer southern countries of Europe, such as Portugal, Greece and Yugoslavia than to the north of Italy.

Engineering, construction and textile manufacture are Italy's three most important industries. Turin and Milan in the north are both very industrial cities. Turin is the home of Fiat, Europe's largest car producer. Like other European manufacturing industries throughout the 1980s, it cut back its workforce, and increased its use of automated production equipment.

At the same time, Olivetti, another famous Italian company, changed from being a maker of typewriters to become Europe's second largest Information Technology company.

Financial support from the government in Rome and from the EC have done little to improve the situation in the *Mezzogiorno*. It still suffers unemployment twice that of the north. It creates only a quarter of the country's wealth, but has 36 per cent of Italy's population.

Industrial wealth is focused in the north of Italy.

24

Right **An efficient European transport network makes trade between European countries possible.**

There is a final point to be made about how the way we run our industries affects life in Europe. Due to improvements in working and living conditions, and because of the advancement of medicine, the Western European population is living longer. The taxes paid by working people are having to support more and more people who don't work: children, the elderly and the unemployed.

Industry, in both Eastern and Western European countries, has led to many improvements, but also posed some big problems. We must look to the Europe of the future to ensure that industry helps improve the quality of our lives, including those of us both in and out of work.

Transport and communications

During the Industrial Revolution two hundred years ago the transport of anything was slow, and made international trade difficult. Roads were poor, although canals allowed for the movement of heavy raw materials. Communications and trade were speeded up by the introduction of railways in the 1840s.

Since the Second World War, the development of a European motorway network has encouraged the rapid movement of raw materials, semi-processed and finished articles to different markets across the continent.

A rapid and efficient European transport network, combining road, rail, air and sea has enabled producers to make their goods in countries or regions where property prices and wages are lower than elsewhere, whilst still being able to send their goods to the markets quickly.

The telecommunications industry (telephones, fax machines, computer links, satellites and TV) has speeded up the communication of information between people and countries.

The market 'The market place' is traditionally a spot where goods are bought and sold. Today, 'the market' means the kind of customers who want to buy a particular product. Buying and selling is explained in more detail on page 26.

Below **Radars gathering information at an airport. Without its communications technology, European industry would not be able to compete effectively with the rest of the world.**

25

Industry and trade

Trade is all about buying and selling. It is no good for a manufacturer to make things if nobody wants to buy them. He or she would soon go out of business. So if making the goods is one side of the coin, selling them is the other. Trading goes on at many different levels. There is domestic trade, within one country, and there is international trade, between different countries.

In today's society, people sell their time in exchange for money. This allows them to buy the things they need, but have not produced for themselves, such as food, clothing, housing, along with other material goods and services. Manufacturers use advertising to persuade us that we don't just want to buy their latest products, but that we actually need them too.

In Western European countries, goods are seldom sold by the producer directly to the consumer. There are the 'go-betweens' who form a supply chain between the factory and high street shop. This leads to two kinds of trade: wholesale and retail.

Generally, a manufacturer will sell large quantities of mass produced goods to a wholesaler who stores them, selling them at a higher price and in smaller quantities to shops (the retail trade). Retailers make their cut of the profit by charging us, the consumers, more than they paid the wholesaler.

Imports and exports

One country will often specialize in producing things that it is good at making. The goods can range from raw materials like crude oil, natural gas or fish, to finished articles like cars, computers, or even wine.

These packages have been imported from Britain and are being unloaded at Iceland's Reyjavik harbour.

These goods can be exported, bringing money into the country.

Such income then gives a country money to buy in from abroad other things it needs, but doesn't produce for itself. For example, most European countries do not produce their own tea.

These imports increase the choice of goods available to the customer, and raise the standard of living in European countries.

Many European countries have a reputation for specializing in exporting particular products.

The Scandinavian countries of Sweden, Norway and Finland have developed successful paper and timber industries, based on their sub-Arctic conifer forests. The rolls of paper are sold to newspaper companies throughout Europe. In addition, Norway is developing its offshore fields of natural gas. The gas is then sold abroad. Sweden is known for its steel production, and Finland for its high-technology industries.

The USSR is going through a long and painful process of reorganizing its economy. It lacks the money to buy many imports and is looking for increased support from Western Europe, which has agreed to increase its import of Soviet goods.

In the meantime, many Eastern European countries, like Bulgaria and Poland, continue to rely on supplies of Soviet oil from Siberia. Like those exports from the USSR, the nature of future Eastern European exports remains to be seen, and will only become clearer as the countries move from Communist to market economies.

Germany, too, is struggling to reorganize the industry of its former Communist Eastern part. Germany has a very high reputation abroad for quality cars, engineering and chemicals.

Switzerland is still known for its cuckoo clocks, even if its banking industry is internationally much more important! The Netherlands provides something of a transport service for other European countries, carrying goods up and down the River Rhine. Rotterdam's Europoort is the world's largest port, and the point where many imports enter Europe before distribution.

Belgium is the European headquarters for many multinational corporations, and along with Britain, is an important centre for international banking.

French cars and wine are known the world over. The same is true of Italy. Both countries also have successful high-technology industries.

The Greek shipping fleet is one of the largest in the world, while Spain and Portugal manage to import millions of sun-seeking tourists every year!

Above **The Port of Aegina, Greece. The Greek shipping fleet is one of the largest in the world.**

Right **Some European countries restrict the sale of foreign goods by placing a tax on them. This Cannon camera costs far more in Europe than in Japan, the country where it was produced.**

Free trade and trade restrictions

In theory, countries trade openly and freely between each other, exchanging the best of what they produce, without any restrictions. This is called free trade. In reality, however, a government or trading organization can always take political decisions to limit free trade in one of three ways.

1. It may decide to subsidize its own industries. A subsidy allows goods to be sold abroad more cheaply than they would otherwise be, allowing them to compete with similar but cheaper goods produced elsewhere. The EC has practised this policy and has subsidized its agricultural products when exporting them elsewhere. This has led to angry protests from other countries in the world, like the USA, who want to see free trade being practised everywhere.

2. Governments may want to protect their domestic industries from foreign competition by increasing the price of cheaper imported goods with a tax called a tariff. This is because cheap imports can destroy the market for one's own home-produced goods, causing firms to go bankrupt and people to become unemployed. Again, the EC has sometimes used tariffs to protect its textile industry from South-East Asian competition, and its electronics industry from Japanese competition.

3. The third way of restricting trade is to enforce a quota, limiting the number of things imported into a country. Before the Single European Market, Italy and France imposed a quota on Japanese cars imported into their countries. This was to protect their own car manufacturers, like Fiat and Citroën, from Japanese competition.

Comecon and Eastern Europe

Countries in the same region, or which share similar ideas, often club together to improve trade within the group and protect themselves from external competition. Europe has had three main trading organizations: the Council for Mutual Economic Aid (COMECON), which existed until 1991, the European Community (EC) and the European Free Trade Association (EFTA). Between them, all the countries in Europe are represented. Telling the story of their aims and development also tells the story of Europe's industrial and economic development since the Second World War. This chapter examines the first of these organizations, COMECON.

After the Second World War came the Cold War, a period of mutual mistrust and hostility between East and West. It was caused by political differences between the Communist countries of the USSR and Eastern Europe on the one hand, and the capitalist countries of the USA and Western Europe on the other.

After the war, East and West had to rebuild their shattered countries. Western Europe received a lot of financial help from the USA under a scheme called the Marshall Plan. Otherwise, it was feared, former West Germany and other countries would come under Soviet control, as had already happened to East Germany, Poland, Czechoslovakia, Hungary, Bulgaria, Romania and Yugoslavia.

The creation of COMECON was the Soviet answer to the West's Marshall Plan. COMECON was set up by the Communist countries of the USSR and Eastern Europe in 1949 to increase industrial output and create a common market for trade. Because COMECON chose not to trade with capitalist countries, it remained outside the rest of the world economy.

Under COMECON, the Eastern European countries changed to a system of central economic

One very obvious sign of the start of Russia's westernization was when McDonald's was finally allowed to open a store in Moscow.

Above **Inefficient planning and transport in the Soviet Union meant that shops were often starved of food supplies. Today the situation has not really changed, despite moves towards a market economy.**

Below **Germans from former East Germany now have to cope with the prospect of unemployment, something which in the past most Eastern Europeans were sheltered from.**

planning. There were no private companies, and everything was owned by the State which decided what to produce, how much, and where to produce it.

The aim was to become self-sufficient in all things, and to create a wealthy society for the good of all by expanding industrial production. The countries industrialized very rapidly. A series of Five Year Plans laid out the production targets for key industries, particularly iron and steel.

Central economic planning eventually proved to be inefficient. It led to shortages of some products, even basic food and household necessities, and produced surpluses of other

things. By the 1980s it had become very hard for the authorities to prevent their populations from knowing about and envying the higher standards of living in neighbouring capitalist Western European countries. Whilst Western European industry began to change (using computers, more automated machinery, and making a start on preventing pollution), industry in Eastern Europe became increasingly old-fashioned, inefficient and harmful to the environment.

Forty years of Cold War ended in autumn 1989, with peaceful revolutions in Eastern Europe. After the initial joy, and the election of democratic governments, Poland, Hungary and Czechoslovakia are seeing more clearly the harsh problems facing them. In particular, these countries are now facing the reality of unemployment, something which under their former Communist governments they had not had to deal with.

With the end of Communism in Eastern Europe, COMECON no longer had a purpose. It stopped trading in 1991. The Eastern European countries now no longer look to the USSR for economic help, but to the EC, and to the West.

Attempts to attract Western European money to support Eastern European industries have

The changing face of Polish industry

In the late 1940s when Poland became a Communist country, its industries were taken out of private hands and were put under State control. Since the end of Communism in autumn 1989, however, the new democratic government has been trying to reverse this situation. There has been a lot of talk in the West about the triumph of capitalism over Communism. The reality, though, is much more difficult.

Poland is trying to change its old centrally planned command economy to a Western style market economy. The change is so difficult to bring about, that Poles are now worse off than they were before.

Under Communism, Poles had little money and nothing to buy. Yet in these early years of democracy, wages have gone down, and food prices have gone up. All sorts of expensive Western goods are available in the shops, but nobody has any money with which to buy them.

In the past, 90 per cent of Polish industry was owned by the State and 75 per cent of Polish workers were employed by heavy industry, such as coal, steel, ship building and vehicle production. Under the old system, the State-run companies did not have to make a profit, nor did they pay any attention to the environment.

The acid rain over the industrial city of Katowice is the worst in Europe, because of pollution from the burning of coal. Polish rivers are also the most polluted in Europe.

Today, Polish companies have to make a profit, yet nobody wants to buy poorly-designed, badly-built articles. Hence, many of the large, old industries are closing down. Unemployment is increasing. Poland is looking towards the EC for economic assistance, but this has been slow in coming. There is still a long way to go before Poland feels the benefits of the changes it is making.

led to huge and rapid change. Polish industry, for example, will have to become as modern and competitive as that of Germany or the Netherlands. This has meant that many factories have been closed, and thousands of people have been made unemployed, before the industries are rebuilt, using hi-tech modern Western production methods.

When Western industrialists have gone to invest their money in Eastern European factories, their idea has been to make goods cheaply, by paying the workers much less than they would get in the West. With such low input costs, profits will be all the greater when the goods are sold in the West. It is a difficult period of change for Eastern Europe, as they shift their societies from Communist to capitalist ones.

The EC and Western Europe

An important step on the road to post-war peace and reconstruction in Western Europe was the foundation in 1951 of the European Coal and Steel Community (ECSC). Industry and wealth could not be rebuilt without large quantities of coal, iron and steel, since so many other industries, like car manufacture, rely on these basic goods.

The control of important iron and coal reserves on the French-German border in Alsace-Lorraine had long led to tension between the two countries. By encouraging co-operation in the production and trading of coal, iron and steel, the ECSC helped avoid conflict.

The organization worked so well that the ECSC's members, known as 'The Six', (the three Benelux countries Belgium, the Netherlands and Luxemburg, and Italy, France and Germany) decided to co-operate in the production and trading of other goods. This led to the creation of the European Economic Community (EEC) in 1958, now called the EC.

The basic idea of the EC is that the general standard of living is improved by increasing industrial production, and strengthening trading links between the member states. Together these member states make up a 'Common Market' where their products can be sold. Some people in the EC believe that one day, political unity in Europe will follow on from economic co-operation.

The EC has certainly succeeded in encouraging industrial growth and increasing trade. Between 1958 and 1987 trade between EC member states increased eight times. Trade with countries outside

Industry and advertising go hand in hand, with companies keen to persuade the public into buying the latest products.

Orange-growing is still a major source of income for Spain.

Industry in Spain

Spain has long been separate from the rest of continental Europe. This ended in 1975 with the death of General Franco, the dictator who was responsible for the isolation of his country. Spain began to look outwards again, and increased its trade with the rest of Europe. In 1986 it joined the EC.

Spain is very much a country made up of different regions, each with its own strong identity. Those in the north, like the Basque country and Catalonia, are much more industrialized than the poorer, agricultural southern region of Andalucia, or Galicia in the north-west.

Heavy engineering and ship building grew up in the Basque port city of Bilbao, its expansion supported by the nearby coalfields. On the Mediterranean coast, Barcelona also became an important industrial centre, noted for its textiles. During the Spanish 'economic miracle' of the 1960s these regions became ever more industrialized. However, both cities were hit very hard by the oil price rises in the 1970s. Increased production costs led to fewer sales. During the early 1980s many businesses went bankrupt, and thousands of workers were made unemployed.

Those companies which survived have reorganized. Cotton factories in Barcelona are now using fewer workers, and some of the most modern automated equipment in the world. The Spanish steel industry has also reorganized along similar lines. Together, chemicals, metal products, machinery and transport equipment account for about 50 per cent of Spain's exports.

Spain's largest service industry is tourism. The resorts along the Mediterranean coast attracted 45 million tourists in 1990, mostly from northern Europe. Tourism provides 10 per cent of the country's wealth, and jobs for 1.2 million people.

the EC increased 3.5 times.

Co-operation between member states is not limited to industry and trade alone, but covers farming, finance, social services and legal systems as well. What is known as the Social Charter seeks to improve the rights and welfare of workers throughout the EC.

The Single European Market

The Single European Market (SEM) has redrawn the map of Europe by removing the internal trading

Germany since 1945

In 1945 at the end of the Second World War, Germany lay in ruins. Now it is Europe's richest and most industrialized country. After the USA and Japan, it is the third most industrialized country in the world. How did this transformation occur?

It has been said that 'Germany and Japan lost the war, but won the peace'. They had to start all over again, and rebuild their industries from scratch. They replaced them with the most up-to-date factories. Germany's largest industrial firms show what the country is good at: traditional manufacturing industry. Daimler-Benz and Volkswagen produce motor vehicles, Siemens make electrical goods, and BASF, chemicals.

With the reunification of East and West Germany in 1990, however, came many difficult problems. Compared to the West, East Germany's industry is old-fashioned and inefficient. Bringing it up to Western standards has led to the rapid closure of many industrial companies. Three million people were made unemployed within a year, nearly half the workforce.

Western money is being used to support new industry in Eastern Europe. If the change in economic systems from Communism to capitalism is successful, the new Germany will be standing at the heart of a new Europe.

frontiers which existed between the EC's member states. Enclosing a population of 341 million people, it is the largest single free market in the world. Goods, people, services and money can freely move and trade within the market.

Creating the Single Market has not been easy. With twelve member states, there have been twelve different sets of trade barriers to remove, such as taxes and tariffs which limit the import and export of goods between one another. Hundreds of laws have had to be passed to create it. Besides removing tariffs, common agreement has had to be made on other things like safety standards, and whether or not taxes should be placed on goods.

It is likely that the Single Market will lead to greater specialization in the production of goods. Britain and Germany are world leaders in the chemicals industry, so there is no point in countries such as Greece, for example, trying to compete with them.

Spain, however, can manufacture cars for half the cost it takes to produce them in Germany, so it is likely that more German car manufacturers will build assembly plants in Spain. The winners are likely to be the industrialized countries of northern Europe, not the more agricultural ones of the south.

Large trading countries outside Europe, such as Japan and the USA, are concerned that with the

Single Market, the EC will close in on itself, and restrict imports from outside. They call this situation the development of a 'Fortress Europe'. They have attempted to side-step this problem by buying up certain European companies, so that they are already present inside the 'Fortress', and have access to its large, profitable market. For example, the Japanese car manufacturers Honda own a share of Rover, the British car company. IBM, the large American computer company has a presence in every EC country. Cars made in Germany by the American manufacturers, General Motors, go by the name of Opal.

The European Free Trade Association

The European Free Trade Association (EFTA) was set up in 1960 as an alternative to the EC. Its aims were much the same: to improve the standard of living of member countries by increasing free trade amongst themselves. Once again, the way of achieving this was to reduce trade barriers, taxes and tariffs between members.

Britain, Denmark, Norway, Sweden, Switzerland, Austria and Portugal were EFTA's first members. Later, Finland and Iceland also joined. Denmark and Britain, however, left EFTA to join the EC in 1973, as did Portugal in 1986. Because of the wider changes going on in the whole of Europe, EFTA itself is going through many changes during the 1990s.

Sweden, Switzerland, Austria and Finland did not take sides with either the USA or the USSR during the Cold War. Since it has ended, they no longer feel it is necessary to remain neutral. Because of this, it is likely that EFTA's remaining members will one by one join the European Community.

Industrial wealth is not evenly divided between EC countries. At present, Portugal is one of the EC's least industrialized members.

35

Profiles of industry

As has been said earlier in this book, Europe is one of the world's major industrial powers. A wide range of goods is produced in European countries and exported all over the world. Some of the most important European industries include the production of electrical and electronic goods, and the chemical, car, food and paper industries. Areas which are not so important or are in decline include timber, machinery, footwear and clothing, textiles, iron and steel, and ship building. This chapter will look at a selection of these industries.

The construction industry is just one of the many hundreds of European industries.

ELECTRONICS

Just think for a moment of all the different electronic goods which you probably use every day, ranging from a digital watch to a video. Our high standard of living in Britain is supported by consumer electronics, which are used in the home. These range from solar-powered pocket calculators, to personal stereos, hi-fis, compact disc players, TVs, videos and camcorders. The big new development in the 1990s is high definition television (HDTV), providing clear pictures. 'White goods' describes things like microwaves and washing machines. Some of the goods help save time, and others help improve our leisure time.

The electronics industry also supports several other very large industries. The computer industry is rapidly changing as European, American and Japanese manufacturers compete with each other to bring out new models and win new buyers. The telecommunications industry provides telephone, fax and satellite links around the world. The large European weapons industry uses microelectronics in 'smart missiles', which are guided by computer.

The European Community saw the importance of the electronics industry at an early stage during the 1970s. Electronics has been seen as a new industry with a bright future, which is why it has been called a 'sunrise industry'. It has provided new economic growth, outside the old regions with their declining 'smokestack industries' of coal and steel. However, although the electronics industry creates a lot of wealth, it does not employ a workforce anywhere near the size of the traditional manufacturing

A modern European office, with employees using computers, telephone headsets and photocopier.

industries it was expected to replace.

American and Japanese companies have set up bases in Europe, and are competing with European manufacturers within the Single Market. All three competitors hope to sell their electronic goods to the Eastern European countries when the latter's economies become stronger.

IRON AND STEEL

During this century, a large and successful iron and steel industry was essential for the development of many other European heavy industries, such as ship building and car production. However, by the late 1960s many newly industrialized countries (NICs), for example South Korea, Taiwan and Brazil, were producing steel more cheaply than was possible in Europe. This led to a situation where there was more steel available on the international market than anyone ever wanted to buy. Prices fell, and by 1975 there was a crisis in the European iron and steel industry.

The EC's response was to 'restructure' the industry, in other words, to close many steel plants, and make thousands of steel workers unemployed. Steel production was cut from 167.5 million tonnes in 1974 to 125.9 million tonnes in 1987 (although that figure is once again

Steel: The main producers	
(figures in millions of tonnes)	1989
Belgium	10.9
France	19.3
Italy	25.1
Netherlands	5.7
Spain	12.7
UK	18.8
W Germany	41.1
European Community	**138.6**
Turkey	7.7
Europe outside EC	25.1
Japan	107.9
US	88.4
Brazil	25.0
South Korea	21.9
Canada	15.4
India	14.4
South Africa	9.5
Taiwan	8.6
Mexico	7.7
Australia	6.7
WORLD TOTAL*	**480.4**

*includes other producers

Sources: IISI, Economist Intelligence Unit forecasts

increasing). These drastic measures made the industry profitable once more.

The bar chart shows that more than 80 per cent of steel in the EC is produced by only five member states: Germany, Italy, France, Britain and Spain. The EC produces more steel than either the USA or Japan.

Above **The largest steel works in Spain are in Barcelona.**

Right **An engine is lowered into the front of an Aston Martin car.**

MOTOR VEHICLES

It simply is not possible to talk about the European car industry, without connecting it to the wider world of car production. And that means Japan and the USA.

On the one hand, there are truly European manufacturers like Fiat of Italy, and Mercedes-Benz of Germany. On the other hand, there are multinational corporations that sell their cars all over the world. For example, Japanese companies like Nissan, and American ones like Ford make and sell their cars in Europe. How 'European' is a car like the Rover Montego, which contains both British and Japanese parts?

Earlier this century, every European country produced its own cars. The building of American cars in Europe started as long ago as the First World War. By the 1970s large numbers of Japanese cars were being imported into Europe. They sold so well that they are here to stay. Japan continues to increase its share of car sales in Europe and the world, challenging European and American manufacturers.

Before the Single European Market, Italy and France were able to protect their own car manufacturers, such as Fiat and Peugeot, from Japanese competition by importing only a small number of Japanese cars. Not any more. Nissan, Toyota and

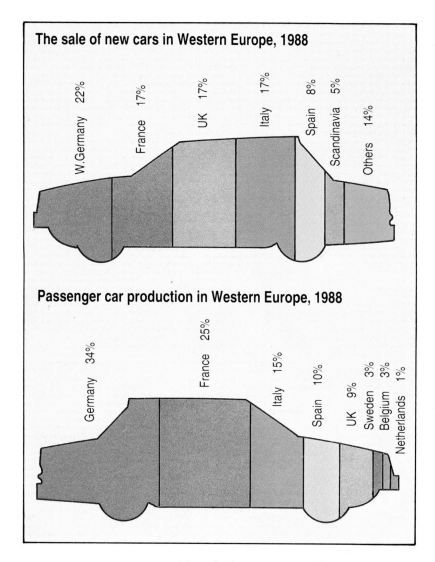

The sale of new cars in Western Europe, 1988

W.Germany 22%
France 17%
UK 17%
Italy 17%
Spain 8%
Scandinavia 5%
Others 14%

Passenger car production in Western Europe, 1988

Germany 34%
France 25%
Italy 15%
Spain 10%
UK 9%
Sweden 3%
Belgium 3%
Netherlands 1%

Car production in Eastern Europe

Picture two cars standing side by side. One is a Trabant, made in former East Germany, spluttering out dirty exhaust fumes. Its bodywork is made of laminated board, and its engineering dates from the 1950s. The other is a BMW, made in former West Germany, its engine running quietly on unleaded petrol. It has a sporty aerodynamic profile, and the latest in car accessories and engineering.

The image shows the difference not only between the East and West European car industries, but between East and West European industry as a whole. They have been light-years apart in terms of design and efficiency.

Since the end of the Cold War, Western car manufacturers have set up production in Eastern Europe. American, Japanese and West European car producers hope that when the Eastern European countries modernize, and become richer, they will want to buy far more of their cars.

Honda have set up factories in Britain. From here their cars can be sold anywhere within the Single Market because they are made in the EC.

Europe has long had a high reputation for luxury cars made by Mercedes, BMW, Jaguar, Porsche and other companies. They too, are being challenged by a new series of luxury Japanese cars.

Above **The Italian
company Benetton
runs visually
stunning advertising
campaigns, and
successfully sells its
clothes in many
European countries.**

Left **Until very
recently, Trabants
were the most
popular cars in what
used to be East
Germany. In 1991
Volkswagon bought
the company up with
the idea of
modernizing the
design of the car.**

TEXTILES

Until the 1950s and 1960s France
and Britain commanded the world
trade in textiles. That situation
changed when Hong Kong, Taiwan
and other countries began to sell
cheap textiles on the world
market. European companies
could not produce cloth as
cheaply, so nobody bought it.
Many firms went out of business.

One way of keeping some of the
industry alive was to cut
production costs by reducing a
large workforce and using more
machinery. One quarter of all EC
textile workers were made
redundant between 1980 and
1987, and many more automated
spinning and weaving machines
were introduced.

Like the French and British
textile industries, the cotton
industry of northern Spain was
also badly affected by cheap
South-East Asian imports. The
closure of many companies was
accompanied by the
unemployment of manual workers.
After getting rid of one-third of its
workforce in the early 1980s, Spain
too invested in the most modern
automated equipment.

. With fewer workers, and more
machinery, the Spanish textile
industry began to make profits
once again. Working alongside
popular and fashionable designers,
stylish Spanish clothes have
regained their place in the market.

Benetton

Benetton is an example of an
Italian textile company which has
successfully ridden the wave of
change. It has done this through
its use of Information Technology
and automation.

The electronic cash-registers in
every Benetton fashion store are
linked by computer to the
company's factories in Italy. Every
day they feed back information on
sales. Changes in what people like
and dislike can be quickly spotted.
The flick of a switch on the
production line means more
jumpers of the desired colour and
style can be produced and sent
out to be displayed and sold in the
shops.

Great Britain

In the nineteenth century Britain was known as the 'workshop of the world'. But in 1983, for the first time since the Industrial Revolution, Britain began to import more manufactured goods than it exported. The USA, Japan, former West Germany and France had already overtaken British industrial output. Why did this decline in manufacturing industry occur?

One reason is that British industry was struck very hard by the economic recessions of 1973 and the early 1980s and 1990s. When the cost of goods went up, many companies could not afford to keep going. They either closed down, or made large numbers of workers redundant. The major traditional manufacturing industries like iron, steel and ship building were hit especially hard. So were Britain's main industrial regions: the north of England, southern Scotland, South Wales and Northern Ireland.

Service industries like banking and insurance in the south of the country have become more important than manufacturing industry. British Steel and other companies began to make profits once more only by cutting back their workforce and increasing their use of automated production equipment.

Whilst British manufacturing industry may have declined, many American and Japanese manufacturers, such as Nissan, have been attracted to Britain.

There are a number of reasons for this. The British government has offered such companies grants to base themselves in regions of declining industrial importance, such as South Wales and the north-east of England.

British workers are well-trained, but are paid less than their German or Dutch counterparts. This allows the foreign company to make larger profits than it would if the goods were produced in that company's home country.

Thirdly, once established in Britain, these foreign companies have a firm foothold within the whole of the EC. With the Single European Market, this means that Japanese cars produced in Britain have easy access to the rest of the EC, and can be sold anywhere within its borders.

CHEMICALS

The European chemical industry is a world leader. Eight of the world's top ten chemical companies are European. Four of these are German (BASS, Hoechst, Bayer and Ciba-Geigy), one British (ICI), one British-Dutch (Shell), one French (Rhône-Poulenc) and one Italian (Mont Edison). Plastics, pharmaceuticals, fertilizers and paints are just a few of the products made by the industry. Without chemicals, the wheels of manufacturing industry would stop turning. Because the chemical industry is so important to other industries it has not suffered as badly as iron or steel.

Many chemical products are

An 'industrial sunset' over a European chemical plant. Sometimes it is hard to imagine that the objects we use everyday are the result of many manufacturing processes. The production of plastics, for example, involves chemicals which can be harmful to the environment if not treated properly.

based on oil and natural gas. From these raw materials a range of basic chemicals such as ethylene and propylene are produced. These chemicals are known as 'feedstocks', and provide the basic ingredients for many other chemicals.

Although the European chemical industry is tightening up its control of pollution, the industry has been responsible for some ecological disasters. In 1986 a fire at the Sandoz chemical plant in Switzerland sent 30 tonnes of agricultural chemicals into the

Rhine, and killed everything in the river north of Basle.

Pollution also results from the use of fertilizers and pesticides by the farming industry. Carried into rivers by rainwater, these chemicals find their way into drinking water, where even tiny quantities can be harmful over a period of time. At the moment it is the consumer who pays for improvements in water quality, but some environmentalists argue that it should be the chemical industries.

The future

European industry, like Europe itself, is going through many changes. This is nowhere more true than in the USSR and Eastern Europe. Time will tell how these former Communist countries adapt to Western-style market economies. Trade competition between the USA, Japan and the EC will continue to increase, as each industrial power looks for new markets around the world for its products, and new ways of making profits.

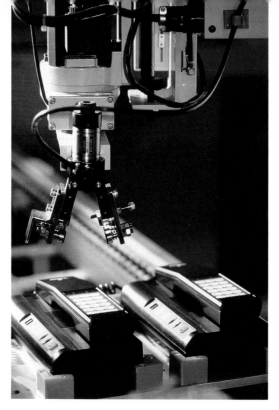

European industry also faces challenges from newly industrialized countries such as Brazil and Taiwan. In order to be able to compete with their cheaper goods, production costs have to be kept down. This is leading to the increased use of automated equipment, and fewer workers being employed in manufacturing industry.

Increasing concern for the environment means that industry cannot ignore the pollution of the air, land and seas that it causes.

Whilst we as Europeans enjoy a high standard of living, we must not forget that there are still many parts of the world which are very poor indeed. It is the responsibility of Europe and the developed countries of the world to use our wealth and industrial might not just for ourselves, but also for the good of others.

Top **The mass-production of plastic phones. Modern hi-tech industry appears very clean and precise, but it is important to look at the hidden costs of our consumer industries. When we buy things we should make sure that the quality is high and that the objects will last.**

Bottom **We depend on our environment for everything, including all types of industry. We must look after Europe's seas and lands, for they provide our future.**

Right **The formation of the EC.**

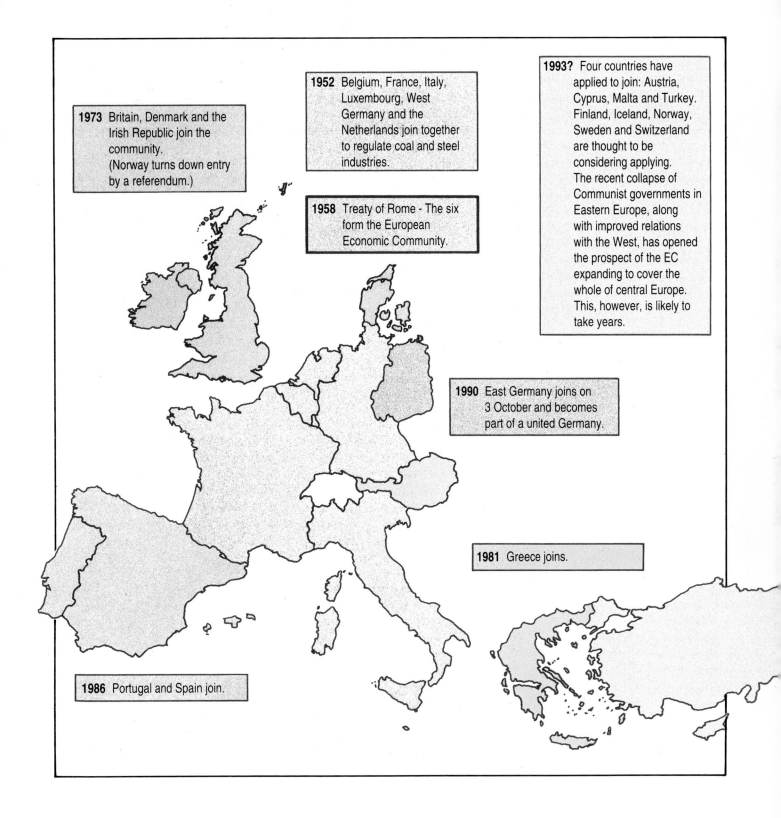

1973 Britain, Denmark and the Irish Republic join the community.
(Norway turns down entry by a referendum.)

1952 Belgium, France, Italy, Luxembourg, West Germany and the Netherlands join together to regulate coal and steel industries.

1958 Treaty of Rome - The six form the European Economic Community.

1993? Four countries have applied to join: Austria, Cyprus, Malta and Turkey. Finland, Iceland, Norway, Sweden and Switzerland are thought to be considering applying.
The recent collapse of Communist governments in Eastern Europe, along with improved relations with the West, has opened the prospect of the EC expanding to cover the whole of central Europe. This, however, is likely to take years.

1990 East Germany joins on 3 October and becomes part of a united Germany.

1981 Greece joins.

1986 Portugal and Spain join.

Glossary

AUTOMATION The use of computers to control machinery and increase productivity.

CAPITALISM An economic theory that believes in private property, and believes that individuals should be free to become wealthy by making and selling things for a profit.

COMECON The Council for Mutual Economic Aid. This was set up in 1949 by the Communist countries of the USSR and Eastern Europe to increase industrial output and create a common market for trade. The Council ended in 1991.

COMMAND ECONOMY The old Communist way of controlling the economy through central state planning.

COMMUNISM An economic theory which believes that the state should control the major industries on behalf of the public.

ECONOMICS The way in which a country creates wealth and uses its resources.

EUROPEAN COMMUNITY (EC) Consists of Belgium, France, Italy, Luxembourg, Germany, the Netherlands, Britain, Denmark, the Irish Republic, Greece, Portugal and Spain (see page 45).

EUROPEAN FREE TRADE ASSOCIATION (EFTA) Established in 1960 to eliminate trade tariffs on industrial products; consisted of Britain, Denmark, Norway, Sweden, Switzerland, Austria and Portugal. Finland became an associate member in 1961 and Iceland joined in 1970. Britain and Denmark left EFTA to join the EEC in 1972.

HIGH-TECH INDUSTRY Industries which use a lot of automated equipment, like electronics.

INDUSTRIALIZATION The rapid development of manufacturing industry brought about by the introduction of machinery.

IT Information Technology. The use of computerized information to help increase a company's output.

MARKET ECONOMY The capitalist way of controlling the economy by allowing individuals and private companies to make and sell things for profit. Also known as free enterprise.

MECHANIZATION A phase of the Industrial Revolution when machines were introduced to increase productivity.

MULTI-NATIONAL CORPORATIONS Huge international companies which produce and sell their goods all over the world.

NICS Newly Industrialized Countries, for example Taiwan and Brazil which industrialized in the 1970s.

PRODUCTIVITY The measurement of an industry's efficiency. Often the number of goods produced by each worker.

QUOTA A fixed share or amount.

RESTRUCTURING The reorganization of industry. It has led to increased automation and a smaller workforce.

SMOKESTACK INDUSTRY The traditional heavy coalfield-based industries of iron, steel and ship building.

SUBSIDY Government money used to keep the cost of goods down.

TARIFF A tax on goods passing from one country to another.

Books to read

The subjects of industry, trade and economics are discussed on the news and in the newspapers every day. So is the European Community.

The EC publishes its own leaflets and books. *Europe in Figures*, 1988, is very useful, and available from the Information Office of the European Communities. The *Financial Times* frequently publishes detailed surveys of different industries. At the beginning of each year it publishes a review of European industry.

If you would like to find out more general information about certain European countries, Wayland has published a series of books called 'Countries of the World'. It includes Britain, France, Greece, Italy, the Netherlands, Spain and West Germany.

The useful books listed here tackle subjects relating to industry.

Baker, Jeannie: Window (Julia MacRae Books, 1991)

Becklake, John: Pollution (Franklin Watts Ltd, 1990)

Bender, Lionel: Invention (DK Eyewitness Guide, 1991)

Elkington, John, and Hailes, Julia: The Young Green Consumer Guide (Victor Gollancz Ltd, 1990)

Lambert, Mark: Focus on Iron and Steel (Wayland, 1987)

Lekachman and Van Loon: Capitalism for Beginners (Writers and Readers, 1981)

Matthews, Rupert: Twentieth Century Industry (Wayland, 1989)

McConville, Brigid: The Role of Trade Unions (Macdonald, 1986)

Parker, Steve: How Things Work (Kingfisher Books, 1990)

Pizzey, S., and Snowdon, S.: The Computerised Society (Wayland, 1986)

Ross, Stewart: Towards European Unity (Wayland, 1989)

Rowland-Entwistle, Theodore: Focus on Coal (Wayland, 1987)

Further information

If you are doing a project on European industry, there are many ways of collecting more information. If you are interested in a particular country you should write to its embassy in London. Many large industrial companies have education departments. Most of the organizations listed here will send you free leaflets about what they do.

BP Educational Service
PO Box 5
Wetherby
West Yorkshire
LS23 7EH

Chemical Industries Association
Publications Department
Kings Buildings
Smith Square
London
SW1P 3JJ

Ford Motor Co Ltd
Public Affairs – Room 1/187
Eagle Way
Brentwood
Essex
CM13 3BW

Information Office of the European Communities
8 Storey's Gate
London
SW1P 3AT

Index